KU-265-563

Bright Ideas

Drama

Written by Jane Fulford, Merryn Hutchings, Alistair Ross and Helen Schmitz

Contents

Published by Scholastic Publications Ltd,
Marlborough House, Holly Walk,
Leamington Spa, Warwickshire CV32 4LS.

© 1990 Scholastic Publications Ltd

Written by Jane Fulford, Merryn Hutchings,
Alistair Ross and Helen Schmitz
Edited by Christine Lee
Sub-edited by Catherine Baker
Illustrations by Jane Bottomley
Artwork by Liz Preece, Castle Graphics,
Kenilworth.

Printed in Great Britain by
Loxley Brothers Ltd, Sheffield

Front and back covers designed by Sue
Limb, puppets made by Mary Lack,
photographed by Martyn Chillmaid.

4 INTRODUCTION

10 NAME GAMES AND WARM-UPS
Starting with names   11
Greetings   12
Wiggling   13
Stretching and curling   14
Follow my leader   15
Huggy three   16
Pass on the sound   17
Just a minute   18
Guess who spoke   19
Word tennis   20
Good news, bad news   21

22 DEVELOPING TRUST
Walking and running   23
Who's your partner?   24
Moulding into shape   25
Mirror images   26
Puppet and puppeteer   27
Blind walks   28
Pendulums   29

30 MIME
Travelling light   31
What's in the box?   32
Hot potato   34
Expressing emotions   35
What's my job?   36
Give us a clue   37
Machines   38
Mime a story   39
The Rocky Monster Show   40
Silence   41

42 IMPROVISATION AND ROLE-PLAY
Developing voices   44
Parties   45
Party arrivals   46
Crossed lines   47
First lines   48
Props   49
Bible stories   50
Proverbs   51
Sounds different   52
Persuasion   53

Circle improvisation   54

56 DILEMMAS
Library books   57
That's our bus!   58
Possession   59
The broken lock   60
Accident or design?   61
Lost: one sick-note   62
Late home   63

64 MEDIA DRAMA
The Price is Right!   65
Winner   66
Advertisements   67
Television news   68
On screen   70
On the air   71
Sports reporter   72
News story   73

74 HISTORICAL DRAMA
Personally speaking   75
Suffragette   76
An inspector calls   77
Evacuees   78
Castle building   79

The Home Guard   80
Car ride   81
Exploration   82
Team effort   83

84 WORKPLACE DRAMA
Hats   85
Working corner   86
Delaying tactics   87
What's my line?   89
Health and safety   90
Accusation   91
Shop complaint   92
Production line   93
Job interview   94
Hard sell   95

96 SHIPWRECKS AND DISASTERS
Scene-setters   97
Shipwrecked!   97
Aircrash   98
Lost in space   99
Developing the action   100
What shall we rescue?   100
The first day   101
Sharing out the jobs   102

Who needs rules?   103
Time out   104
Lean times   105
Swap shop   106
Who's in charge?   107
Treasure trove   108
The great escape   109

110 PERFORMANCE
I liked that play   111
Treading the boards   112
It's a myth   113
Puppet show   114
The moral is . . .   116
Assembly   117
Musical thoughts   118
A wider audience   119
Opportunity knocks   121
Drama festival   122
Freeze!   123

124 REPRODUCIBLE MATERIAL

128 OTHER SCHOLASTIC BOOKS

Introduction

WHY DRAMA?

In drama, children draw on their observations and experience of the real world in order to create a make-believe world. By creating, developing and reflecting on this make-believe world, they can come to understand more about themselves, their friends and families, and the real world in which they live.

- They can think about how people behave in particular circumstances by exploring a variety of social situations.
- By acting out emotions, they can explore a range of human feelings.
- Drama can help children to explore choices and moral dilemmas; they can make decisions which, in the course of the drama, are tested out, and can be reflected on afterwards. This can give them confidence as decision-makers and problem-solvers in the real world.
- They can represent different points of view, and test their individual viewpoints against others. This can lead to exploration of conflict, negotiation and resolution.
- Children can gain self-confidence through taking part in classroom drama.
- Drama develops children's ability to work together in groups, trusting and relying on each other. They begin to appreciate the part played by each individual within the group.

At first children's dama may be superficial and action-oriented, but you can help their work to grow in depth by offering guidance and timely intervention, and by encouraging them to reflect on and discuss what they have done.

DRAMA ACROSS THE CURRICULUM

Drama can be an integral part of work in many curriculum areas, from core and foundation subjects such as English, history and geography to cross-curricular themes such as economic and industrial understanding and citizenship.

Drama can play an important part in the development of spoken language, as it allows children to use language in a wider range of social situations than would normally arise in the classroom. They can use language for a wide variety of purposes: for example, to persuade, challenge or appease. Role-play also involves children in collaborative talk.

Drama helps children to understand the people around them and the social world in which they live. It can also help children to understand other peoples and societies, both historical and geographical.

In drama children use both their imaginations and their experiences of the world. In this respect drama has much in common with art, music and dance. These areas come together particularly in putting on a performance.

WAYS OF WORKING

Children's first experiences of drama usually involve role-play. Teachers can encourage development at this stage by providing different settings and props, for example in the home corner.

Story-telling also has close links with drama. Bring stories to life by telling them dramatically, using sound effects and appropriate voices for the different characters. You can also enhance them by using props or puppets. The teacher is the role model; if you tell stories in a dramatic way, children in your class are more likely to pick up these skills.

Many of us were put off drama in our childhood because it was seen as 'a performance' for an assembly or an end of term play. Performance has a role to play in drama, but it should not be the only, or indeed the main, form of drama. Children should have regular opportunities to take part in classroom (or workshop) drama. This does not have to be a specially timetabled session, but could be developed from the classroom work in other curriculum areas.

You will need to build up the children's confidence carefully. Within the class, all children can become involved at their own level and within their own capacity. They should not be forced to join in or be 'put on the spot', but it should be easy for them to join in a structured and unthreatening activity.

Begin sessions with a physical warm-up activity, such as stretching and bending, or a voice warm-up. Involve all the children by gradually building up the size of working group.

- Start with activities which are carried out by individuals working within the larger group (for example, *Travelling light* or *What's my job?* on pages 31 and 36).
- Next, introduce activities which involve pairs of children working together (for example, *Delaying tactics* on page 87). Try to ensure that children do not always work with their best friends. *Huggy three* (page 16) is an activity which encourages children to get quickly into groups of different sizes, and this can be used to form groups for a drama session.
- Then let the children try working in fours or in larger groups. This demands greater skills of co-operation and negotiation (for example, in *Accusation* on page 91).

You will also need to consider the nature of the improvisation. It is less threatening for children to act out stereotypes or roles which are not directly related to themselves. For example, they will find it easier to explore conflicts in which they take on the roles of adults at work, than to act out classroom events. It is only when the group has developed mutual trust, confidence, and an ability to reflect that they can tackle situations in which they may be directly involved, such as bullying, the new child in class, and so on. Even then, these areas will need to be tackled with considerable sensitivity on your part.

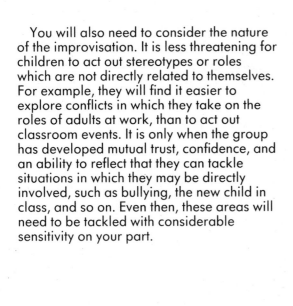

PRACTICALITIES

The activities in this book were written with a primary class in mind; however, they would also be suitable for a school drama club.

Many of the activites need plenty of space, and may be best carried out in a hall or large room. Others can take place in the classroom, and children may feel more confident when working in their own room with less fear of interruption.

Most of the activities need very few materials. It is a good idea gradually to build up a collection of props. Simple props often help a child to assume a role. You could collect a variety of hats, scarves, gloves, sunglasses, walking sticks and so on. Telephones are also useful.

THE STRUCTURE OF THIS BOOK

This book is divided into sections. Some focus on a particular type of activity, such as warm-ups, mime or improvisation. Others are thematic, such as workplace drama or historical drama.

The book includes some structured activities which may be particularly suitable for teachers and children who are new to drama and who lack confidence. It also includes open-ended activities which could be tackled by more experienced classes and teachers.

Name games and warm-ups

You may be working with a class with which you are unfamiliar or starting a new drama club, so some name games are included in this chapter to help you and the children get to know each other.

Drama sessions should generally begin with a warm-up. The purpose of this is to relax everybody physically and mentally, and to reduce anxiety and inhibition. Possible warm-ups include stretching and relaxing, voice exercises, and activities to encourage members of the group to feel relaxed with each other.

Starting with names

Age range
Five to eleven.

Group size
Whole class or large group.

What you need
Enough space for the class to sit on the floor in a circle.

What to do
Ask the children to sit down in a circle. Introduce the activity by explaining that everyone is going to say their name and a food they like eating; for example, 'My name is Rita and I like eating spaghetti bolognaise.' Introduce yourself, then let each child do the same. When each member of the group has introduced himself, go round the circle again, and encourage the children to try to remember everyone's names and foods.

Now introduce the child sitting on your left: 'This is Frank and he likes eating mangoes.' Ask that child to introduce his neighbour, and so on round the circle. When a child cannot remember the correct name and food, ask the neighbour to introduce herself again, so that everyone has a chance to learn the name.

Then ask each child to introduce the child sitting on their right in the same way. As the children become more confident in recalling names and foods, make it more difficult by introducing the child sitting, say, five away from you round the circle.

Continue the activity until most children can remember most of the names and foods.

Greetings

Age range
Five to eleven.

Group size
Whole class.

What you need
Space for the whole group to move around.

What to do
Let the children walk round the room, weaving in and out of the spaces. Encourage them to shake hands with each child they meet, greeting them by name.

Then ask the group to choose three parts of the body with which to greet people instead of a handshake: for example, they could greet the first person they meet by rubbing noses, the second by touching feet, and the third by touching shoulders. Let each person proceed in their own sequence of movements using nose, foot and shoulder. Thus eventually some pairs will be greeting each other by touching the shoulder of one to the foot of the other. They should still greet the other child by name.

After a while, introduce three more parts of the body, thus making a six part sequence.

This activity works well in breaking down some of the barriers of self-consciousness and embarrassment.

Wiggling

Age range
Three to eleven.

Group size
Whole class, preferably standing in a circle.

What you need
No special equipment.

What to do
Ask the children to wiggle their fingertips, then continue through the arms by moving the wrists, the elbows, and then the whole arm in windmills. Ensure that they isolate the different parts of the body and move them one at a time. Encourage them to move their shoulders up and down, alternately if possible, then drop their heads forward and roll them gently from side to side.

Then ask the children to wiggle their toes, again trying to move the different parts of the body separately, moving the ankles and knees, rotating the legs from the knees and finally shaking the legs.

Next, get them to flop over like a clown, so that their hands touch the floor (or as near as possible), and gently bounce up and down. Let the children repeat this two or three times, breathing out as they flop over and breathing in as they stand up straight.

Finally, ask the class to jump up and down, wiggling and shaking as many parts of the body as possible so that everybody is relaxed and warmed up ready to start.

Stretching and curling

Age range
Three to eleven.

Group size
Whole class.

What you need
A large floor space.

What to do
This is a simple exercise for beginning or ending a drama session.

Ask the children to find a space and lie on the floor. Then ask them to stretch their bodies, and then curl up. Next ask them to stretch again, in a different direction, and then to curl up in another way.

Repeat this a few times, constantly encouraging the children to think about the directions of their movements and their curling positions. Choose one or two children to demonstrate.

What to do

This activity forms a good warm-up to a drama session. To begin with, take on the role of leader yourself. Ask the class to line up behind you, and when the music starts, lead them around the room, leaping, jumping, turning, crawling through the legs of furniture, sliding along the bench on your stomach and waving your arms. Use large exaggerated movements; many children will reduce the scale in their imitation, but the object is to get them moving with freedom and confidence.

After a short time, ask the child immediately behind you in the line to take over as leader while you go back to the end of the line. Continue like this until everyone has had a go at being leader.

Follow my leader

Age range
Five to eleven.

Group size
Whole class.

What you need
Plenty of space, a tape recorder, a cheerful piece of music, a few obstacles such as a bench, chairs, stools, mats.

15

Huggy three

Age range
Five to eleven.

Group size
Whole class.

What you need
A large space, tape recorder, taped music.

What to do
Ask the children to walk or jog around the hall, weaving in and out of each other, making use of all the space. Tell the children that when you call out 'huggy' followed by a number, they quickly have to form themselves into groups of the appropriate size, and hug the other members of their group. They then move round the room again until the next number is called.

Use music, making this a version of musical bumps, so that each time the music stops the children have to form 'hugs' of whatever size you call out. This is essentially a co-operative activity, not competitive. There is no need to eliminate children who are left out on any occasion. Try to call out numbers which will divide the group evenly, so that usually nobody is left out.

This activity generally results in children being less fussy about the companions they pick. It is a good way of mixing everyone up, and shaking up normal patterns. You can end up by calling 'huggy' followed by the group size you want for the next activity, so that everyone is encouraged to work with different people in the class.

Pass on the sound

Age range
Five to eleven.

Group size
Whole class.

What you need
Space to sit in a circle.

What to do
This warm-up activity focuses on sound. The idea is to pass different sounds around the circle. For example, start by saying 'Aaah', looking at the child sitting on your right. Ask her to continue the 'Aaah' sound, and pass it on to her neighbour, so that the sound is passed round from child to child.

Try passing different sounds, exploring the sounds of vowels and consonants. Talk about the different sounds. What shape is your mouth when you make the sound? What does the sound remind you of? Is it short or long? What sort of film would it make a good sound effect for?

Follow-up
Play Zoom-eek. Start with the sound 'zoom', making a noise like a racing car. Each child in the circle repeats 'zoom', until someone decides to say 'eek', which represents the squeal of brakes. This reverses the direction of the zoom – until someone else says 'eek' and sends it back again. Limit each player to one 'eek' when you play this game, otherwise children can keep the game in one small area of the circle.

Just a minute

Age range
Five to eleven.

Group size
Whole class or smaller group.

What you need
A stopwatch or watch with a second hand.

What to do
Tell the children that you are going to ask them to speak continuously for a fixed period of time. Older children may be able to manage a minute, but this will probably be too long for younger ones, or for the first attempt. Suggest a subject such as playtime, my best friend or what I did in the holidays.

Let the children all speak simultaneously the first time you try this activity. This ensures that everyone has a go, but no one is publicly embarrassed by their inability to keep going.

Later, give children advance warning to prepare a speech on a topic of their choice. Introduce some additional requirements, such as no hesitation, repetition or getting off the subject.

Guess who spoke

Age range
Five to nine.

Group size
Whole class.

What you need
No special equipment.

What to do
Ask the class to sit together on the floor. Choose one child to go to the far end of the classroom and hide her eyes.

Point silently at one of the other children, who should then greet by name the child who has her eyes shut; for example, 'Good afternoon, Nita'. Ask the first child to rejoin the group and guess who spoke.

Next, ask the child who spoke to hide his eyes.

Word tennis

Age range
Five to eleven.

Group size
Whole class, working in pairs.

What you need
No special equipment.

What to do
Ask two children to take it in turns to say as many words as possible relating to a given subject, without repetition or hesitation. They could, for example, state children's names in turn.

When they come to a halt, ask two different children to take on the game, either continuing with the same subject, or introducing a new theme. The idea is to encourage quick thinking.

Themes could include parts of the body, books you've read, names of cars or sports.

Good news, bad news

Age range
Seven to eleven.

Group size
Whole class or smaller group.

What you need
Space to sit in a circle.

What to do
This activity works on the same principle as a circle story-telling activity; each child in turn adds a sentence to the story. But in this case ask children to begin their contribution with, 'the good news is' or 'the bad news is'.

Encourage the children to make their good or bad news relate to what the previous child has said. Sometimes this will be too difficult, in which case the good or bad news should be related to the general story-line which is being built up. It may help to start the story yourself, to build up a setting with many possibilities. For example:

Teacher: This is a story about Jane and John and their parents, who live in a tiny house in a tiny village in the back of beyond, and are very unhappy.
Child A: The good news is they are about to move to a much bigger house.
Child B: The bad news is that although the new house has a lot of rooms, each room is even smaller than the rooms in the old house.
Child C: The good news is that the family have been given some shrinking powder so that each one of them will shrink to two feet tall.
Child D: The bad news is that all their food is kept in a wall cupboard six feet high and they can't reach it . . .

This activity encourages children to listen to what the person before them has said, and to respond to it. These skills are important in workshop drama. As the children become more skilful you can refine the rules, so that they cannot simply reverse the contribution of the previous child. For example, Child D above could not have said, 'The bad news is the shrinking powder didn't work.'

Developing trust

It is important in drama that the participants trust each other, and this will take time to develop. Taking part in drama makes many people feel vulnerable. Children are generally far less inhibited than adults, but many of them feel worried when asked to perform in front of others. Activities to develop trust are particularly important with a new group, just beginning to work together. By developing trust children are more able to work collaboratively and to rely on each other.

Walking and running

Age range
Three to eleven.

Group size
Whole class.

What you need
A large space.

What to do
Ask the children to walk around the room, weaving in and out of the spaces and being very careful not to bump into anybody. Then ask them to increase their pace from jogging to running as fast as possible, still avoiding contact with anybody. Then ask them to slow down gradually, first jogging, then back to walking, and finally coming to a halt.

Next let the children walk backwards slowly, again weaving in and out, and increase the pace as before. Repeat the process, slowing down and then stopping.

Repeat the whole process, forwards and backwards. This time ask the children to keep their eyes closed. Make sure that safety is a priority.

Follow-up
This warm-up activity encourages trust within a group. Follow it up with 'Blind walks' and 'Pendulums' on pages 28 and 29, which develop the same theme.

Who's your partner?

Age range
Five to eleven.

Group size
Pairs.

What you need
Sufficient space for everyone to sit comfortably on the floor.

What to do
Ask the children to sit with a partner and to discuss 'things they like'. Leave them for a short while, then ask them to sit back to back. Ask one child from each pair to describe her partner.

Some children will describe their partner's physical characteristics, others may describe his or her personality. Either way is acceptable, although you must take care that the descriptions do not become too personal. This is particularly good for a group of children who are new to each other.

Follow-up
Work on developing the descriptions as a group.

Moulding into shape

Age range
Five to eleven.

Group size
Pairs.

What you need
Large space, tape recorder, taped music.

What to do
Ask the children in each pair to decide who will be 'A' and who will be 'B'. Explain that A is going to be a lump of Plasticine or clay, and that B is going to mould A into something. Their 'models' do not have to resemble anything in particular. It helps to play some gentle music while the children are experimenting with their models.

When the children have been working well together for a few minutes, ask the 'B's to stand back and admire their 'works of art'. Then ask the 'A's to move round the room without altering their positions! Some will find it harder than others. Then let the pairs reverse the roles.

Follow-up
Let the children work with clay. Continue in pairs and let the children make real models of each other.

Mirror images

Age range
Five to eleven.

Group size
Pairs.

What you need
Enough space for everybody to sit on the floor.

What to do
Ask the children to sit on the floor facing their partners. Let one child lead while the other copies his actions in a mirror image.

At first, ask the children to move their hands and arms only, but after a while encourage them to move their legs as well. However, stress that they must retain eye contact at all times, and must not look away. This activity should be carried out in silence, to encourage concentration.

Once the children have developed some confidence, and can work without giggling, encourage them to develop a repeated routine based on about five different movements. Let them practise this, and then demonstrate it to the group.

Ask the children to sit back to back, and repeat the routine and demonstrate again.

Follow-up
Discuss together the difficulties and differences the children have encountered: the importance of eye contact and, when that is not possible, the importance of body contact.

26

Puppet and puppeteer

Age range
Seven to eleven.

Group size
Pairs.

What you need
No special equipment.

What to do
Ask the children to work in pairs, facing each other, with one child as a puppet and the other holding the imaginary strings. Ask the child holding the strings to indicate how the puppet should move. Encourage them to start very slowly, one arm or leg at a time, and to keep the movements synchronised so that the puppet responds to every movement of the strings, and stays still when the strings are not moved.

Let the pairs change round so that each child has a turn at controlling the movements as puppeteer, and a turn at responding as the puppet.

Follow-up
This is a good preliminary to other drama activities which explore power relationships.

Blind walks

Age range
Five to eleven.

Group size
Pairs.

What you need
An open space or hall.

What to do
Organise the group so that one member of each pair closes his eyes tightly, and the other one leads him round the room, weaving in and out of the other children. The guide should take care to keep his partner safe, avoiding crashing into furniture or other people. Then ask the pairs to swap, so that both children have a turn at being blind and at leading.

At first the guides will probably give lots of instructions and information to their partners. Comment on how helpful this is, but then encourage the children to try working in total silence.

Tell the children to change partners and work with someone different. Now ask them to repeat the activity, but this time touching each other only by the very tip of one finger. Encourage them to work in silence. Let them change round so that all the children have tried out both roles, leader and led. Get the children to talk about how it feels to be led by a fingertip.

Finally, while the children are leading each other round the room, ask them to change partners without the 'blind' partners opening their eyes. Can they manage this? Often two 'sighted' children will walk off together leaving their 'blind' partners together with no leader!

Follow-up
Continue to develop trust between children in the class by introducing 'Pendulums' (page 29). This activity also makes a good preliminary to 'Exploration' (page 82).

Pendulums

Age range
Nine to eleven.

Group size
Threes.

What you need
A large space.

What to do
Ask two children to stand facing each other, with the third in the middle.

To begin with, ensure that they stand as close to one another as possible, because the children on the outside are going to push the child in the middle gently forwards and backwards in a pivot or pendulum action. Explain that the one in the middle must remain straight, rocking on her feet rather than from her hips. Emphasise that it is the pushers' responsibility to look after the middle child, and not to let her drop.

This activity needs to be performed in silence because it demands concentration and trust.

When the children have developed more expertise, encourage them to move apart so that there is more room for the pendulum movement.

Never move the children too far apart, or they could drop the child in the middle.

Follow-up
Discuss the nature of trust; the children's feelings when being rocked and the feelings of those doing the rocking. This eventually develops into a very relaxing process. You could develop this by having a group of

children in a circle pivoting one child in the middle. At all times it is important to maintain concentration, silence and safety.

Mime

Mime focuses children's attention on body language; they use their bodies to communicate instead of words. Facial expression, use of hands, and the whole attitude of the body are important.

Mime is an important dramatic skill, and activities which concentrate on this aspect are useful to draw children's attention to it.

Travelling light

Age range
Five to eleven.

Group size
Whole class or large group.

What you need
A large space.

What to do
Ask the children to move across the room in different ways. Tell them to imagine moving under the following conditions:
● Walking through a river where the water comes up to your knees;
● Standing on a huge green jelly that covers the floor of the hall;
● Walking through water in boots that are too big and keep coming off;
● Crossing the street in heavy traffic;
● Crossing a beach in the face of a gale;
● Carrying a small mouse with a broken leg.

Next, divide the children into small groups and brief each group as to how they are to move. Get the rest of the class to guess what they are doing. This can lead to constructive criticism and positive suggestions as to how the movements can be improved.

Follow-up
In small groups, ask the children to act out what they find at the end of the journey. Can the other children guess what it is? This activity can introduce the idea of building a performance round a story.

What's in the box?

Age range
Three to eleven.

Group size
Whole class.

What you need
A large space.

What to do
Begin the activity yourself by miming a box. It may be large, small, narrow or tall, but you must consider the item that is to be found in the box. First outline the shape of the box, and then start to open it; it may have ribbons, bows or adhesive tape, which you can indicate in your mime.

Once you have opened the box, mime what you have found. This could be a delightfully furry kitten, a slimy snake or a maggot-ridden apple; your reactions should demonstrate exactly what is in the box.

Ask the children to guess what is in the box, and when they have guessed correctly, return the item to the box and then smash the entire box in any way you like; perhaps by jumping up and down on it! Then ask the child on your right to repeat the process, making up his own ideas of 'what's in the box'.

Continue repeating the mime around the circle, without uttering a sound! Only those who are guessing may talk.

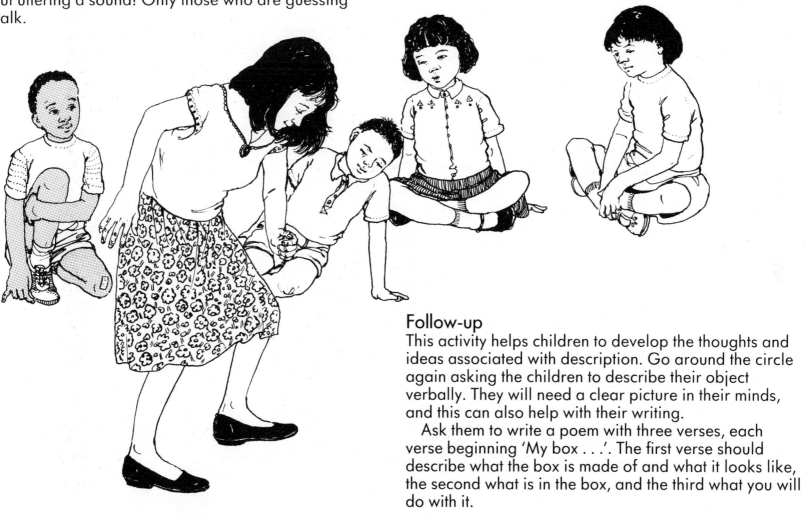

Follow-up

This activity helps children to develop the thoughts and ideas associated with description. Go around the circle again asking the children to describe their object verbally. They will need a clear picture in their minds, and this can also help with their writing.

Ask them to write a poem with three verses, each verse beginning 'My box . . .'. The first verse should describe what the box is made of and what it looks like, the second what is in the box, and the third what you will do with it.

Hot potato

Age range
Three to eleven.

Group size
Whole class.

What you need
A large space.

What to do
Ask the children to mime eating different foods such as spaghetti, an apple, an ice-cream cornet, soup, a hot potato. Then suggest that they mime preparing foods; chopping onions, peeling carrots and so on. Then introduce other ideas, such as hammering, drilling, hoovering, or any activity which the children can mime actively, working on their own.

As the children will be working individually, they will need plenty of space. However, they will be doing their mimes simultaneously so that no individual is performing to another. This helps to build confidence, because no one is singled out to perform.

Follow-up
Go on to develop mime work further, for example in 'What's my job?' (page 36).

Expressing emotions

Age range
Five to eleven.

Group size
Whole class, working individually.

What you need
A large space.

What to do
Give each child a different feeling or emotion, such as happiness or sadness, and ask them to move around the room in a manner that expresses these emotions.

Give older children words such as angry, ecstatic, desperate, frightened, indifferent, hysterical, malicious, confused, miserable, haughty, sceptical, and so on. (A thesaurus might help!)

It is more difficult to express complicated emotions such as indifference and scepticism than it is to act out straightforward emotions such as happiness and anger. However, it is important that children come to grips with their emotions, especially as increasing demands are made of them in role play.

Follow-up
Continue to develop emotions in role play, using activities such as 'Parties' (page 45).

What's my job?

Age range
Five to eleven.

Group size
Whole class.

What you need
No special equipment.

What to do
Ask the children to sit on the floor in a circle, as an audience. Then perform a mime showing a person doing their job, such as an artist, a writer, a window cleaner, a snooker player, an athlete, a disc jockey, etc. Ask the children to guess who it is, and continue the mime until somebody guesses correctly.

Invite any child who would like to do a mime to continue. It is very important that you do not pressurise the children into miming; let them develop at their own pace. You can carry on this activity for as long as you like, depending upon the children's enthusiasm and expertise.

Give us a clue

Age range
Seven to eleven.

Group size
Whole class or smaller group.

What you need
No special equipment.

What to do
This version of charades, which follows the rules of the television game *Give Us a Clue*, is generally popular with children, and encourages some very inventive mimes. Many children are familiar with the programme and its conventions, so this activity is usually easy to organise!

Ask the children to take it in turns to mime the title of a book, film, television programme or song to the rest of the group, who try to guess what it is. Let the children think of the subject of their mimes themselves, but ask them to whisper it to you or another appointed chairperson who can see fair play.

Encourage the children to use appropriate actions to indicate whether their mime will be a book, film, song or television programme (for example, by drawing a rectangle in the air for television or winding a camera for film). Ask them to hold up their fingers to show how many words are in the title. They can mime the whole title, or take it one word at a time. Words can also be broken down into syllables which can be mimed individually (the number of syllables being shown by fingers held against the left arm).

Let the rest of the group call out guesses for each word or syllable and for the whole title. The mimer should indicate whether the guesses are correct, incorrect, or nearly right.

Let the person who guesses correctly provide the next mime, but if they have had a turn already ask them to hand it on to someone who has not.

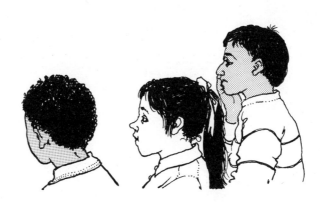

Machines

Age range
Three to eleven.

Group size
Whole class.

What you need
A large space.

What to do
Talk about machines, discussing those with which the children are familiar. Ask children to work individually and mime a machine, then ask them to choose another machine and mime that, adding sound effects.

Next let the children work in pairs to develop another machine, again using sound effects.

Ask them to get into groups of four, this time making a more complex machine. Finally, let them work in groups of eight to form a machine that makes something. This could be ice cream, cut glass or tomato ketchup; usually the children come up with exciting ideas!

Follow-up
Get the class to design a new machine. It could be a time machine or a machine to help in the home or garden. Ask the children to draw their machine and make a model of it, working individually or in groups.

Mime a story

Age range
Five to eleven.

Group size
Groups of three or four.

What you need
Books and newspapers for reference.

What to do
Encourage the children to tell each other stories in small groups. They may tell about 'what happened on the way to school', or retell a well-known tale, or describe a story which is currently in the news. Go around the groups and listen to some of the stories.

When the story-telling is coming to a close, ask each group to choose one of their stories and mime it to the others. Remind them that they must present all the important parts of the story, so they might need to structure it into separate scenes. Again, go around the groups to help them with their ideas.

Follow-up
Choose another story from the story-telling session, but this time ask one of the group to narrate the story while the others mime the action.

The Rocky Monster Show

Age range
Seven to eleven.

Group size
Groups of eight to ten.

What you need
A large space.

What to do
Explain to the groups that they are to make themselves into 'stone monsters' with each child forming a different part of the creature. Let them practise making the shapes of the different parts of the body. Can they make a shape like an eye or an ear? A mouth with a tongue? How will they build up the main body?

Let one child lead each group and direct the other children as they form a composite whole.

When a good shape has been made, ask the 'monsters' to come to life, eyes opening and closing, arms writhing, neck twisting. Encourage slow deliberate movements. Sound effects can also be added.

Silence

Age range
Nine to eleven.

Group size
Whole class, working in pairs.

What you need
A large space.

What to do
Give each pair a situation around which to improvise a silent drama. Situations could include the following:
● You are cooking chips at home and the pan catches fire. Go to your neighbour and ask to use his phone to call the fire brigade. You have lost your voice and you cannot speak. How can you get your message across?

● There is a dog drowning in the canal, but you cannot reach it on your own. You rush to the nearest person and try to get her to come and help you. Explain, without using any words, what you want her to do.
● You are in the middle of cooking a cake for a birthday party, but you have just dropped an egg on the floor and you haven't any more left. You go to your neighbour's house and explain without using any words what you need and why.

Let each pair act out their silent drama to the rest of the class.

Follow-up
When the children are confident about working in this way, ask them to think of a similar situation themselves and to work with a partner who doesn't know what that situation is. Can the partner guess the problem?

Improvisation and role-play

Improvisation and role-play are important parts of classroom drama. Each improvisation has three main features: firstly, the children take on a specific character or role; secondly, the characters are usually placed in a particular setting; and thirdly, the action will usually be based round a particular incident or event.

● It will be easier at first for the children to take on a stereotype character, but your role as teacher is to help them to progress to an ability to portray more complex characters. Otherwise drama can simply reinforce stereotypes.

● The setting is often based on a real time or place. It results from conscious decisions made by the children or teacher, and to a certain extent determines the action.

● The action often results from a specific incident or event that requires children to interact.

The characters, settings and incidents should all be simple so that the children can concentrate on the fundamentals of the action. The time-scale is often shortened for the same reason.

An important aspect of improvisation and role-play is the discussion which takes place afterwards. Children can reflect on why they made certain decisions, what would have happened if they had responded differently, and so on. This can sometimes be helped by having one or more children to take on the role of observer, who does not get involved in the action. This reflection on the action helps children learn; it is also important that children come out of role together and resume normal relationships.

Developing voices

Age range
Five to eleven.

Group size
Whole class.

What you need
Something to read aloud.

What to do
This is a fun activity which helps children to develop voice projection and characterisation.

Select a piece of writing, which may be a letter or a passage from a book. However, it is important that you choose something that can be read by all the children in the group. If you are working with younger children, choose a song or a rhyme that they all know well.

Ask individual children to read or recite the same piece in different ways. For example, ask somebody to read the piece as a bed-time story for a three year old, or maybe as a political speech. Other suggestions for reading are: as a secret message, a scandalous news item, a piece of gossip, a vicar's sermon, a headteacher's assembly, a television news broadcast, a Saturday morning children's television programme, and so on.

Parties

Age range
Nine to eleven.

Group size
Whole class, working individually.

What you need
A large space.

What to do
Ask the children to imagine that they are at a party. Ask them to think about the sort of person they would like to be.

Give them about two minutes to decide who they are going to be, then tell them that the party has begun, and that they are to introduce themselves to each other by name, and say what they do for a living.

It is important that you take on a role yourself and join in the party. This may simply be the role of host, encouraging partygoers to eat and drink, and generally helping everyone to mingle.

When you feel confident that the improvisation is flowing, freeze the whole group and ask one small group to carry on. Concentrate on continuing their interesting conversation, and then encourage the party to resume.

Follow-up
Introduce themes to help the children extend their role-play and characterisation. Use ideas such as a football supporters' party, a crooks' party, a toffs' party, a teachers' party or a weightwatchers' party.

Party arrivals

Age range
Seven to eleven.

Group size
Whole class, working in groups of four.

What you need
Sufficient space for each group to work in turn, while the others watch.

What to do
Ask one group to develop an improvisation, with the rest of the class as the audience. Encourage the children to listen and participate, being a 'good audience'.

Let one child be the host of a party. Suggest to the other three children that they take on specific characteristics when arriving at the party. These could be, for example, repeating everything twice; behaving like the Prime Minister; being a hypochondriac; a ghostbuster; an alien creature, and so on.

Ask the child hosting the party to guess which characteristics the guests have chosen by interacting with them. He can have assistance from the audience if necessary!

Follow-up
Continue developing improvisation through circle improvisations (page 54).

Crossed lines

Age range
Seven to eleven.

Group size
Pairs.

What you need
Toy telephones, yoghurt pots, toilet roll tubes, string.

What to do
Provide the children with toy telephones. Alternatively, let the children make phones out of clean empty yoghurt pots, the inner tubes of toilet rolls and string.

Give the children subjects to discuss on the telephone. These might be gossip, a complaint, a news item or something related to project work. Get pairs of children to sit back to back so that they cannot see each other as they talk. Pick out one pair with a pre-arranged signal, and ask the others to stop and listen to their conversation for a moment. Are there any amusing juxtapositions? What do the other children think is the subject of the telephone call from the snippet that they have heard?

Follow-up
Discuss the sort of conversations people have on the phone – gossip, delivery of bad or good news, making arrangements for an outing or meeting, complaining about something, and so on.

Get the children to think of a conversation they might have and ask them to hold one-sided conversations into their 'telephones'. Let them practise all together at first, to give them confidence. Then ask one child at a time to talk in front of the others, very briefly. Can the children guess what the conversation is about? How do they make this decision? Conceal the speaker behind a screen. Is it more difficult when the children cannot see the face of the speaker?

First lines

Age range
Seven to eleven.

Group size
Pairs or small groups.

What you need
Space in which to work and move, a selection of 'first lines'.

What to do
Give each group or pair the same first line, such as:
- It's just not fair!
- Why are you late – again?
- You promised not to tell!
- I think I'm being followed.
- I've just swallowed my front door key.
- Where's your little brother?
- What have you been doing to this apple?
- Whoever painted the door that colour?
- Why didn't you tell me about the . . .?

Ask the children to work in groups or pairs to improvise a short story based on their first line. At the end of the session ask each group to act out their story to the rest of the class. See how many different interpretations of the first line emerge.

Alternatively, give each group or pair a different first line, and carry out the activity in the same way.

Follow-up
Try the same activity with last lines:
- Thanks very much!
- I knew there was a ghost in the school attic.

- So that's how the ball crashed into my window!
- And then the pink balloon just floated away.
- I always wear odd socks on Mondays.
- But Mum never knew about the sitting room door.
- We never told anyone about the secret chimney.
- The old dog curled up by the fire and dreamed about his adventure.
- The cook had forgotten to fill the kettle.
- And I never went there again.

Props

Age range
Seven to eleven.

Group size
Pairs or small groups.

What you need
A collection of props such as hats, jewellery, a telephone, fake money, an old diary, a beard and/or wig, a few boxes or containers, white coats, a key, a ticket, shopping bags, briefcases, baskets, empty food packets and containers.

What to do
Give each group or pair of children a few props. Limit the type or number of props that you give a group so that it is not merely a dressing-up session. The props should dictate the type of roles that the children take on. A collection of hats, for example, will give the children clues to their characters. What sort of person might wear a bowler hat, a headscarf, a sports cap, a bobble hat, a felt hat? Who might carry a shopping bag, a briefcase or a basket?

Give each group a setting for their action. The collection of hats could be for a group at a bus queue or in a doctor's waiting room, the bags might be carried by people in a supermarket or at a station.

Explain to the children that they are to use the props to improvise a situation. Allow a short time for discussion so that children have some ideas before they start.

Bible stories

Age range
Seven to eleven.

Group size
Groups of about six.

What you need
Space to work, a book of Bible stories.

What to do
Read and discuss some stories from the Bible. The following make good subjects for drama:
- Daniel and the lions;
- Noah and the ark;
- Moses in the bullrushes;
- David and Goliath;
- Saul and Jonathan;
- Jonah and the whale;
- The parable of the good Samaritan;
- The parable of the talents;
- The wedding at Cana;
- The feeding of the five thousand.

Let the children decide whether to act the stories as they were written or to find modern equivalents. What would happen to Daniel today? Who might be the good Samaritan in a city street? Get the groups of children to perform for the rest of the class.

Proverbs

Age range
Nine to eleven.

Group size
Small groups.

What you need
A collection of simple proverbs, blackboard or large sheet of paper.

What to do
Talk to the children about the old sayings that we call proverbs. Make a list of any that the children know. This might include:
- The early bird catches the worm;
- Practice makes perfect;
- Love of money is the root of all evil;
- A stitch in time saves nine;
- One man's meat is another man's poison;
- When the cat's away the mice will play;
- A leopard never changes its spots;
- Actions speak louder than words;
- Forbidden fruit tastes twice as sweet.

Discuss the meanings of the proverbs. Give each group a proverb, and get the children to improvise situations to illustrate it. Either announce the proverb that is being illustrated, or put the list on the board or a large sheet of paper, and ask the rest of the class to guess which proverb is being enacted.

Follow-up
These proverbs could also be illustrated effectively with puppets.

Sounds different

Age range
Nine to eleven.

Group size
Groups of about six.

What you need
Space in which to work.

What to do
Talk with the children about what happens when someone loses their voice, or when the sound is turned down on the television. What would it be like if we could not converse and had to rely on other sounds only?

Then discuss the kinds of sounds associated with certain events and places, such as a football match, a busy supermarket or a children's party. Get the whole class to make vocal sounds associated with various scenes or events. You might suggest the seaside, a busy street, a place in the country, a storm, a classroom and so on.

Ask the children to choose a subject and to work in small groups using only sounds and not conversation. Let groups perform to the rest of the class, who then guess what the scenes are.

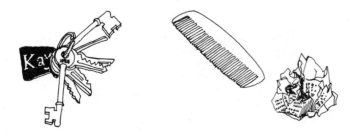

Follow-up
This activity can be extended by using objects around the classroom as sound instruments, such as keys, a comb, a piece of paper torn or scrumpled together. Let the children collect a variety of such objects and make sounds, discussing the scenes or settings in which the sounds they make would be most effective. Try making a sound picture using classroom objects and vocal sounds.

Persuasion

Age range
Nine to eleven.

Group size
Whole class divided into pairs.

What you need
A selection of enticing advertisements from magazines, or a video of a collection of television advertisements, pencil, paper.

What to do
Talk to the children about the selling techniques that are employed by sales people, market stallholders or shop assistants. What makes people want to buy something? Have the children or their parents ever bought something they didn't really want or need? Look at advertisements together and discuss how they are trying to make people buy things.

Ask the children to think of some really useless objects, such as a toeless wellington boot or a car with no wheels. Draw up a list. How would they persuade someone to buy one of these things? After discussion, ask pairs of children to think of a number of persuasive arguments for their product. They toeless boot might be a fashion item that no up-to-date eleven year old would be without or the wheel-less car might be an environmentally friendly vehicle. The children can be as inventive as they like! When they have practised their arguments, get each pair to demonstrate to the rest of the class.

Talk about the job of designing advertisements. Ask the children to pretend that it is their job to design advertisements and they have been asked to promote one of the useless items. What sort of advertisement would they want? Divide the class into small groups and ask them to improvise a television advertisement for a useless item. This work could also include pictures, posters, music and jingles.

Circle improvisation

Age range
Seven to eleven.

Group size
A minimum of ten children.

What you need
Enough space to sit comfortably on the floor in a large circle.

What to do
For this improvisation it is important that you sit on the floor with the children and are part of the circle.

Ask two children to go into the middle of the circle while the others offer ideas for a setting in which they can develop an improvisation. They may, for example, be in a park, on a bus or at a party.

Let the two children begin their improvisation and after a short while, give the command 'freeze', whereupon the children in the middle should automatically stop in their positions. Ask one child to remain 'frozen' while the other returns to her place. Meanwhile, ask the child sitting next around the circle to go into the middle and take over the improvisation.

Try to freeze the situation during a positive movement, such as pointing to the floor, scratching noses or making dramatic arm movements, because this will give a starting point to the child entering the improvisation.

Encourage the new child in the middle to start a different conversation which will alter the setting. She will pick up her ideas from the position of the 'frozen' child. She might say, for example, 'What are you looking for?' or 'Do you think this T-shirt will fit?' or 'Have you hurt your back?'. After a short while, 'freeze' these children and let the improvisation continue around the circle until everyone has had a turn in the middle, including yourself.

Some children might find this rather daunting, but with encouragement they will enjoy developing their techniques of improvisation.

Dilemmas

The activities in this chapter explore situations in which children may be involved in real life. They present the children with choices and moral dilemmas in which they have to decide what to do and say. These activities will need to be handled with sensitivity.

Library books

Age range
Seven to eleven.

Group size
Four or five children.

What you need
A book.

What to do
Explain to the children that they are going to take the roles of members of a family. Two of them should be primary school aged children, but they can decide for themselves on sex, age, interests and so on. Other roles could vary: for example, the teenage son whose main enthusiasm is listening to his records in peace; the mother who is always in a rush, taking on a full time job as well as housework; the grandmother who thinks children should be seen and not heard; and so on. Give them a few moments to decide on their roles.

The scene opens with the youngest child reading. The older sister comes in and says that the book is her library book, and that she wants to read it now. The younger brother claims that it was lying around, and he got it first. The older child says it is too hard for the younger child to read anyway, and so on.

How does the argument go on? What do other members of the family say or do?

When the children have finished their drama, discuss what happened. If different groups were working on the same scene, discuss how the conflict was resolved in each case. Do parents have to sort out children's arguments, or can they do it themselves? Is it better to get a grown-up to propose a solution?

That's our bus!

Age range
Five to eleven.

Group size
Six children.

What you need
No special equipment.

What to do
Ask one child to assume the role of a bus conductor. Tell him that it's getting dark and it's wet, and the bus is full up. He has just had to leave a queue of people behind at the stop because the bus is so full.

The bus is just pulling away from the stop, but is held up at the traffic lights. Two puffing children run up to the platform and jump on board. They are desperate to get home, because their mum has been ill at home on her own all day.

The people waiting at the stop are angry to see the two children jump the queue. The conductor is not pleased either.

What does he say? What do the children say and do? What about the people in the queue?

Possession

Age range
Seven to eleven.

Group size
Four or five children.

What you need
A pencil.

What to do
Ask groups to enact the following scene.

Two children start arguing over a pencil. They each claim ownership, and as evidence say when and where they bought it, when they used it last, and so on.

Let the other children take on the roles of their classmates and the teacher. What do they do about the dispute? Do they intervene? Do they take sides? Do they take on the role of mediator? Or do they just grumble about the noise? What about the teacher? Is she expected to sort out the dispute? Does she?

Situations like this occur in classrooms all the time, and drama provides a good opportunity to reflect on what is going on and on the roles people assume in such disputes.

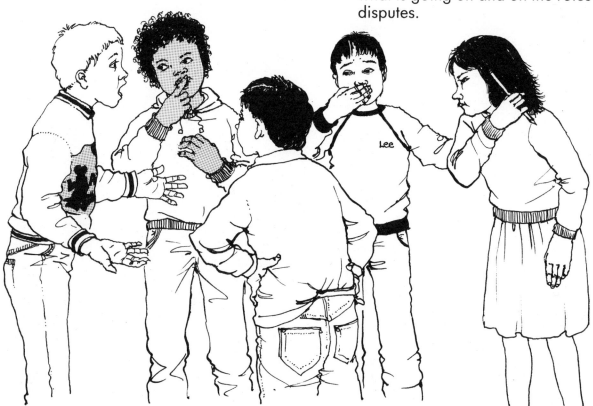

The broken lock

Age range
Five to eleven.

Group size
Groups of three children.

What you need
No special equipment.

What to do
Ask one child to take on the role of a parent who has come to pick up his children from school.

At the beginning of their street, the father gives one of the children the front door key. They both race ahead to unlock the door.

The key jams in the door. There's no other way into the house. There are houses on each side. They know the neighbours are out. All the windows are securely closed.

What do the children do? What do they tell their father? What does he do?

Accident or design?

Age range
Seven to eleven.

Group size
Three or four children.

What you need
A pen.

What to do
Ask the group to act out the following situation.

Two children have been looking round a stationery shop. They have looked at the magazines, the pens and the toys, and have finally bought some sweets. As they

walk away from the shop one of them reaches into her pocket and brings out a pen. She is amazed; she had looked at the pens, but certainly had no intention of picking one up. She must have slipped it into her pocket by accident.

What do the children do? Do they take the pen back to the shop? What does the shopkeeper say? Do they try to replace it without being seen? Or do they take it home and ask their parents to take it back? Or do they just decide to keep it?

Discuss the possible solutions to this dilemma and the reasons for each. Does it really matter if small items are taken from shops when there are so many goods there?

Lost: one sick-note

Age range
Seven to eleven.

Group size
Threes.

What you need
No special equipment.

What to do

Ask each group of three to assume the roles of teacher, headteacher and child, and act out the following situation.

The school has new, stricter rules about children who have had days off. They must bring a note with them from their mum or dad on the first day back, explaining why they were away.

The child can't find his sick-note. Mum certainly wrote it, but did he forget to pick it up? Or did he lose it on the way in?

What should he tell the teacher?

The teacher isn't sure whether to believe the child. She sees the headteacher. What does the teacher say? What does the head do or say?

Late home

Age range
Five to eleven.

Group size
Four or five children.

What you need
No special equipment.

What to do
Ask the groups to act out the following scene.
   A child arrives home from school at about five

o'clock, having been playing with friends on the way.
The mother is furious: she had asked the child to come
home early that day because she wanted to go to the
shops, library or doctor.
   How does the child react? How do other members of
the family react? Perhaps the outing was to buy one of
the other children in the family new shoes. What does
this child have to say?

Follow-up
Discuss the sorts of responsibilities children have to their
parents and vice versa.

Media drama

For most children, television is their main experience of seeing other people engaged in drama. They will take on roles, varying from presenters and newsreaders to characters in soap operas and dramas. It is worth exploring this source of ideas. However, don't assume that all the children in your class have televisions, or that they watch the same programmes.

Newspapers can also be a good source of starting points for drama, both in the nature of the stories printed, and in the interviewing role of the reporter.

The Price is Right!

Age range
Seven to eleven.

Group size
Whole class working in groups of six.

What you need
Copies of the *Radio Times* and *TV Times* (optional).

What to do
Ask each group to prepare an edition of a popular television show: for example, *Opportunity Knocks* or *The Price Is Right*.

Encourage them to act out the behaviour of the host, the assistants and contestants. This usually rather exaggerated behaviour is easy to imitate.

Get each group in turn to present their show to the rest of the class. Encourage audience participation, as most game shows would be very flat without enthusiastic applause and participation.

Follow-up
Discuss sexism in television game shows. Children may already have explored this in their productions by switching the roles of the sexes.

Winner

Age range
Seven to eleven.

Group size
Whole class, working in pairs.

What you need
Tape recorders, or notebooks and pencils.

What to do
Ask the children to work in pairs, as 'A' and 'B'. Brief them on their roles.

'A' is a newspaper reporter who has heard that a local child has won an award. No details are available. 'A' is going to interview the child, and should start thinking what questions to ask.

'B' is the child who has won the award. Ask the 'B's to decide what they have won and what they did to win it; for example, an act of bravery, helping other people or winning a competition. Encourage them to work out the whole story in detail.

After allowing a short time for the children to organise their ideas, get them to act out the interviews. They can all do this at once, pausing occasionally to listen to a particular couple, or the class could act as audience for each interview. Let reporters take notes or tape-record the interview if they wish.

Follow-up
Invite a newspaper reporter to visit the class and talk with the children about preparing for an interview. They could also interview one of the children.

Advertisements

Age range
Seven to eleven.

Group size
Four to six children.

What you need
A video camera and player (optional).

What to do
Discuss the television advertisements with which the children are familiar, and think about what makes them effective.

Let the groups of children make up their own television-style advertisements. They could advertise a forthcoming school event (bazaar, concert, etc) or a product or service they are selling (school T-shirt, school bookshop or product of class enterprise).

The resulting advertisements could be performed as a 'commercial break' in assembly; alternatively you could video them and show them as a continuous loop in the entrance hall for parents.

Follow-up
Discuss techniques used in advertisements to persuade consumers to buy, and talk about issues such as sexism and stereotyping.

Television news

Age range
Seven to eleven.

Group size
Whole class.

What you need
Video equipment.

What to do
Ask the children to devise a news presentation for assembly. This should involve two main newsreaders who present the stories in turn, as on television. There could also be a number of 'on-the-spot' reporters, specialist reporters and interviewers.

The presentation could cover world or local news. The children will have to research the stories they want to present and take on the roles of personalities to be interviewed; for example, the Prime Minister, the President of the United States, a trade union representative, and so on.

Alternatively the class could compile and present a report of school news. This might include interviews with various adults who work in the school and children from other classes.

The whole news report could be presented live, or filmed in advance, and shown on a video. Alternatively, video just some of the interviews in advance and play them at the appropriate moment.

Discuss the ways in which different items are presented, and the neutral role of the newsreader and interviewers.

Follow-up

Discuss how news is collected and selected. Who decides which items are to be shown, and which are the most important? Do all television channels always make the same selections? Watch the news on different channels and compare lists of items and the order of their appearance.

Interview a news editor from a local television station or a local newspaper and discuss these issues.

On screen

Age range
Nine to eleven.

Group size
The whole class, with only a small group at a time using the video camera.

What you need
A portable video camera.

What to do
This activity can be based on many of the drama ideas in this book. Having created various pieces of drama, turn them into a television programme. This may involve rehearsing to ensure that camera crew and actors are clear about their roles, checking audibility, and repositioning characters to face the camera.

A modern video camera is simple enough for a child to use. It will need to be on a tripod, as it will be too heavy for a child to hold for long. Let the children view their work on the television screen, and record the scene again if they are not satisfied. The whole programme could be shown to the school in assembly.

Follow-up
Arrange a visit to a television studio or a location where filming is taking place. Talk with the director and camera operators about their work.

On the air

Age range
Seven to eleven.

Group size
Whole class working in groups of various sizes.

What you need
Radio, tape recorders, cassettes, a tape-to-tape cassette recorder.

What to do
Discuss the sorts of radio programmes which the children like listening to. Let the children listen to a radio programme and comment on the style of presentation.

Ask the class to work in groups to make a radio magazine programme for children, which could include news, drama, music and jokes. Try to make sure that each child has a turn at making up and recording one or more items. Encourage them to speak in the clear and confident voices used by radio presenters, and to avoid long pauses.

Let each group record their own item, then play it to the rest of the class. Ask for constructive feedback. Allow them time to make alterations before compiling the final programme by recording the contributions from each small group, with suitable introductions, on to a single cassette.

The resulting programme could be played in assembly or to another class.

Sports reporter

Age range
Seven to eleven.

Group size
Whole class working individually.

What you need
No special equipment.

What to do
Tell each child to choose a sport they have watched on television or heard about on the radio. Ask them to think about how that sport is reported: constant talk; silences; hushed tones; high pitched gabble; and so on.

Give the children a few minutes to practise reporting a sporting event of their chosen type. Then ask each child in turn to take on the role of sports reporter, and describe their event for the class.

Follow-up
Let the children investigate and imitate the characteristic ways in which other television and radio presenters speak. Newsreaders, for example, aim to use a calm, unemotional and factual tone. Children's television presenters aim for a lively style, making everything fun and exciting. Children may be able to take on the styles of individual reporters they have watched.

Involve the class in an investigation into newspaper stories, looking at and discussing the types of stories used in different papers. Let them pick out those which are suitable for drama. Alternatively, collect the stories yourself, thus avoiding those which you consider unsuitable.

Give each group a story and time to read it. They can then improvise a scene based on the story, and perform it to the rest of the class.

News story

Age range
Seven to eleven.

Group size
Variable.

What you need
A collection of newspapers.

What to do
Collect newspaper stories which children could use as a basis for mini-plays. These could be stories of bravery, reunions with long-lost relatives, building disasters ('the day our dining-room wall fell down'), and so on.

Historical drama

Role-playing historical events allows children to empathise with people living in different times. With secondary pupils, it can be used to get them to look at how and why particular historical characters behaved as they did in a particular crisis. But with primary aged children, the characters involved are often ordinary people, involved in everyday decisions. This allows the children to draw upon their own experiences as a basis for the roles they take on.

This chapter contains ideas for taking on a variety of historical roles. The children will have to undertake some historical research to brief themselves, for example looking at and discussing photographs and period illustrations. All the scenarios suggested here could be extended into more formal drama if you wish.

Personally speaking

Age range
Seven to eleven.

Group size
Groups of four to six.

What you need
Census records of local streets.

What to do
Look at the census records which show who lived in your locality over 100 years ago. Ask groups to take on the roles of families mentioned in the records, or cast the whole class as a series of neighbouring families. Ask each child to establish first the *known* facts about their character, such as their name, age, marital status, occupation and birthplace, and then to research what their life *might* have been like, by reading books and by looking at photographs and engravings of Victorian Britain. Get the family groups to work out their histories: the better they research and plan this, the better the role-play will be.

Devise an incident to start the role-playing: perhaps one of the family loses his job, or relatives come to stay, or there are some newcomers to the street. A Victorian soap-opera will probably develop, as individuals weave their knowledge of life at the time into the known facts about their characters.

Follow-up
If each group is working on a different family, encourage them to bring their stories together.

Suffragette

Age range
Nine to eleven.

Group size
Groups of five to eight children.

What you need
Books and photographs on the suffragette movement.

What to do
Divide each group into two: two or three children take on the role of suffragettes or sympathisers, and the others become those opposed to extending the franchise to women.

Encourage everyone to research the arguments which were used by the suffragettes, and the reasons why they were opposed.

When this has been done, ask one of the suffragettes to make a speech to the rest (perhaps standing on a chair, or even in the open air). Ask the others to encourage her, heckle her or argue with her.

Follow-up
Research further into suffragette tactics, and discuss these with the class.

An inspector calls

Age range
Seven to eleven.

Group size
Whole class.

What you need
Large sheets of paper, rulers, photographs and books about nineteenth century monitorial (sometimes called Lancasterian system) schools.

What to do
Recreate a mid-nineteenth century monitorial school. Arrange tables in rows, and pin up texts for group reading (written in large letters on large sheets of paper) around the walls. If possible raise your desk on a platform at the front of the classroom.

Practise drilling the children to stand up, sit down, and wipe their (imaginary) slates clean on command.

Ask some of the children to be 'monitors', each in charge of a small group of children. Get them to stand their group in a semicircle round one of the reading charts, and tell each child to read out the lines as they are pointed to.

Persuade the headteacher to be one of Her Majesty's Inspectorate. Inspectors used to tour the schools testing children: the teachers were paid on the quality of the children's answers. Usually the testing was through question and answer sessions. Often teachers gave signals to help the children behind the Inspector's back!

Evacuees

Age range
Seven to eleven.

Group size
Whole class, divided into two groups.

What you need
Photographic books on urban and rural life in Britain in the 1930s, luggage labels, two rooms.

What to do
Divide the class in two, and let the two groups go into separate rooms. Tell one group that they are going to take on the roles of country families in 1939. Many of their homes will not have electric lights; some will not have running water.

Tell the other group that they are to be city children, who have never been to the country. Arriving at school one morning, they are told that they are going to be evacuated to the country. Luggage labels with their names are tied to their clothing, and they are marched off to the nearest railway station.

Tell the first group that the city children will be staying with them: they must prepare to receive the guests.

The two groups meet in the evening: the town children have been travelling all day. Let the country families pick the evacuees they will take home. Do the farmers take big lads who can work in the fields? Do others choose girls who will help in the house? What happens? How do the evacuees feel? What do the country people make of their forced guests?

Follow-up
If your school is in a city, try to find local people who were evacuated in 1939. Ask them to talk to the children about their experiences.

If it is a rural school, arrange for a visit from someone who can remember evacuees being billeted in the area. Ask them to describe what it was like to have evacuees in their community. Were the children homesick? What was the attitude of the other children towards the evacuees?

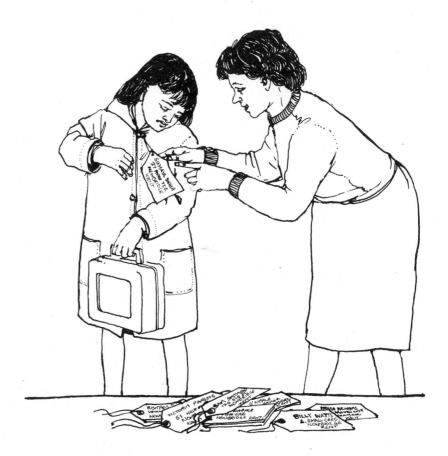

Castle building

Age range
Five to eleven.

Group size
Whole class, divided into smaller groups.

What you need
This activity is suited to a day out in open countryside. Ensure that plenty of adult help is available.

What to do
Tell the class to imagine that they are living hundreds of years ago and need to find a safe place to live. They can farm the land, but need a castle or fortified camp to protect themselves from possible attack.

Where will they build the camp or castle? What sort of area will they look for? Give the groups different tasks; some can look for areas that can be defended, others can look for places that would offer a view of approaching attackers, and others should think about getting water and food. There may be quite a few anachronisms: gently point out any facilities that would not have been available at that time.

Give the groups fairly clear directions about where they can go, and ensure that each group is supervised by an adult.

Ask the groups to re-form, then get them to present their ideas to the whole class and discuss what might be the best place for their castle.

Follow-up
Ask the children to think about how they would organise the building of the castle. What materials would they need? Where would they obtain them? What would the local inhabitants think about the castle-builders?

Let the class plan and build a model castle in school.

The Home Guard

Age range
Seven to eleven.

Group size
Whole class, divided into groups.

What you need
Photographs and stories about the Home Guard in the Second World War.

What to do
Ask the class to imagine that they are the Home Guard in 1940, given the duty of defending the school and its grounds against possible invasion. Encourage them to do some research on the civilian response in the Second World War, and how property was protected. Ask various groups to be responsible for different parts of the grounds.

What will they need to protect? What are the key local facilities? What equipment will they be able to obtain? How will they organise the watching and reporting?

The children will probably be very busy at first, organising and planning. However, once the systems are set up, it will become very routine and boring. Ask them how they feel about the change in pace.

Follow-up
Enhance the role-play by adding fresh information. Perhaps the headteacher is a suspected spy?

Car ride

Age range
Five to eleven.

Group size
Groups of six children.

What you need
Four chairs, a red flag, photographs and stories about early cars.

What to do
Tell the children that they are to act out the first car journey in their area, in about 1900. Let two or three children in each group be car passengers while the others are members of the public. Explain that the cars didn't go very fast anyway, but they were forbidden to go faster than five miles an hour (a brisk walking pace) and had to have a man going in front on foot with a red flag, to warn the public!

Brief the passengers. They would probably have employed a chauffeur to drive for them and to look after the car. They would have been well-off, and the car would not have been able to take them very far as it would have needed refuelling (there were no petrol stations), and the roads were not very suitable.

Brief the public. They have heard of cars, but have never seen one. Explain that people were afraid that cars would frighten farm animals, or injure people.

Set the following scene. The car drives into the area. What do the public think and say to each other? A dog takes fright and runs in front of the car. The car screeches to a halt, and stops with a bang. It won't start again. The dog runs off terrified, as do several sheep in a nearby field.

What does everyone say? Who blames whom?

Exploration

Age range
Seven to eleven.

Group size
Whole class divided into three groups.

What you need
Hall, benches, chairs, mats, transistor radio, paper, pens, blindfolds.

What to do
The activities 'Developing trust' on pages 23 to 29 might usefully be tackled before trying this idea.

Arrange benches, chairs and mats around the hall, forming 'islands' and 'continents'. Let one group become inhabitants of these countries, whose task it is to give explorers information about where they are. This information may or may not be accurate.

Blindfold a group of explorers, and take them into the hall. They should not have seen the arrangements beforehand. Start them off from the door, and play a radio at the door to act as a 'beacon' to guide them back home. Let them explore on their own, and ask them to try to remember where they have been and what they have found (or think they have found).

Ask them to return to the starting point, homing in on the beacon, then take them back to the classroom to exchange notes and to construct a map of their discoveries. Meanwhile, let the next group of explorers begin their trip.

Let groups return two or three times on separate voyages of exploration, modifying their maps in between each trip.

Follow-up
Organise a discussion about what the local inhabitants thought of the explorers (with their repetitive and naïve questions), and how the explorers perceived the local population.

Team effort

Age range
Five to eleven.

Group size
Whole class.

What you need
Various props and costumes, liaison with a local secondary school.

What to do
Arrange for the class to team up with a local secondary school to dramatise an historical event. Let the secondary school pupils act out the roles of principal characters, and the primary school children become groups of villagers, monks, townspeople, or whatever is needed.

There are advantages for both schools, apart from the simple benefits of working co-operatively. The older pupils can take on more detailed and complex roles, while your children will be able to work with many more roles and actors than would normally be possible.

If possible, arrange for the group to work in some historic location, wearing simple costumes.

Workplace drama

Work is central to the way society is organised, and is part of everyday life for adults and children. Children see people at work at home, in shops, on the street, at the doctor's, in school. They are aware of their parents' concerns about work (or lack of work). They use this experience to form ideas and opinions about the world of work.

The way in which many workplaces are organised means that there is generally some conflict of interests between people doing different jobs, and between workers and suppliers, staff and customers. Drama offers an opportunity to explore these relationships and conflicts.

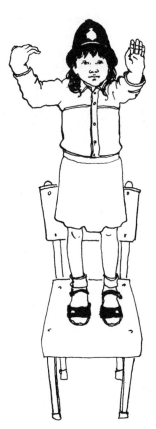

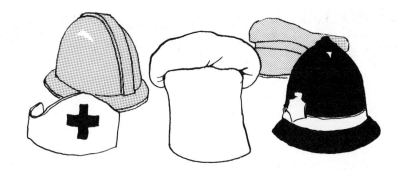

Hats

Age range
Three to seven.

Group size
Individuals or groups.

What you need
A variety of hats worn by people at work (for example police, firefighters, builders, traffic wardens, chefs, jockeys, cricketers, nurses, waitresses), overalls, uniform jackets etc., reference books and pictures of people at work.

What to do
Put a collection of 'work' hats and other clothing in the home corner to encourage role-play. Talk with the children about the work these people actually do. Use pictures and simple reference books as sources of further information.

Follow-up
Invite different workers to visit the class to talk with the children about their jobs.

Working corner

Age range
Three to seven.

Group size
Individuals or groups.

What you need
Suitable equipment to turn your home corner into a work setting, such as a hospital, office, shop, café or workshop.

What to do
Turn your home corner into a work setting. Discuss with the children what it is to be, and encourage them to bring in suitable props. They will need costumes, such as white coats, aprons, overalls, jackets and hats. Toy tool sets or hospital sets and so on can be useful. Use old typewriters (and the class computer if you have one) to make an office setting.

This activity will stimulate role-play of different kinds, and may attract some children who show little interest in the home corner.

Follow-up
Take the children to visit a real work setting like the one they have developed in their home corner. Alternatively, invite appropriate workers to visit the school and talk with the children about their jobs.

house, working on a production line, on a building site, in a shop and so on). Encourage children to think of a wide variety of work.

The other child in each pair wants to have a conversation with the worker. This may be because they do not want to get on with work they should be doing, because they are not working and are free to gossip,

Delaying tactics

Age range
Seven to eleven.

Group size
Whole class working in pairs.

What you need
A clear space, a collection of props to help children get into role, such as hats and suitable implements for various kinds of work.

What to do
Ask the children to develop the following scenario.

One child in each pair is busy working. Ask them to decide what sort of work they are doing (cleaning the

because they are lonely or because there is something genuinely important to talk about.

Allow a while for each pair to decide on the setting for their conversation, and to think about the roles they will be taking up. The workers need to be clear exactly what work they will be doing, and why it is important to get on with it. The conversationalists need to decide what role they are playing, and why they want to talk with the worker. It may help to think about the most talkative people they know!

Ask the workers to start miming whatever work they are involved in, trying to look thoroughly involved in their occupation. Let the 'conversationalists' approach their worker partners and try to get them talking, prolonging the conversation by every possible means. Encourage the workers to try to get rid of the conversationalists so that they can get on with their work.

Let all the pairs do this at the same time. Circulate among them, and occasionally freeze the whole class, asking one pair to continue so that everyone can listen.

Follow-up
Discuss with the class whether this situation ever arises in real life, and, if so, why. What sorts of work are so important that people do not want to be interrupted? Does this situation ever arise in the classroom? What are the best tactics for ending an unwelcome conversation without being rude?

What's my line?

Age range
Nine to eleven.

Group size
Whole class.

What you need
A range of information books about different jobs.

What to do
Involve the children in a quiz game along the lines of the old television panel show 'What's My Line?'. Ask each child to research into different jobs, and select one role for the game. Make sure they know enough about the job to answer questions about it, and that they are able to mime one of the activities involved in the job – preferably one which will be difficult for the other children to guess.

Let the children take it in turns to be the chair, the panel and the worker whose job is to be guessed. Ask the chair to introduce the worker and ask her to mime her job. Then let the panel take it in turns to ask the worker questions. She is only allowed to reply 'yes' or 'no'.

This game can be played in odd moments at the end of the day, until everyone has had a chance to take on each role.

Health and safety

Age range
Nine to eleven.

Group size
Whole class divided into groups of six to eight children.

What you need
Copies of photocopiable page 125.

What to do
Use role-play to examine issues of health and safety at work.

Let the children take on roles of park workers, a union representative for park workers, the park manager and members of the public. Ensure that each group includes one or more park workers, one manager and one or more members of the public.

Give each child the information sheets from photocopiable page 125. These set the scene for a debate about issues surrounding the use of chemical weed-killers in parks. Then let the children take on their roles in groups, and act out the confrontations between the various parties concerned.

Follow-up
Invite local trade unionists to talk with the children about issues of health and safety at work.

Investigate the methods of weed control used in your local park.

Accusation

Age range
Nine to eleven.

Group size
Whole class divided into groups of four.

What you need
No special equipment.

What to do
Ask the children in each group to take on the following roles:
• Factory manager;
• A worker accused of having stolen something from the factory;
• The security guard who has made the accusation;
• A trade unionist supporting the worker.

Ask the children to act out a meeting of enquiry. The worker may have been falsely accused, or have taken the item by mistake. Or he may have taken it deliberately, but not for gain. Or he may in fact have stolen it in order to use it or sell it. Let the children decide.

Follow-up
Discuss the feelings of each member of the group. What is it like to be accused of stealing? What is it like to have power?

Invite a local trade union official to discuss what might really happen in such a situation.

Shop complaint

Age range
Seven to eleven.

Group size
Whole class working in groups of four.

What you need
A collection of props to create a shop scene.

What to do
Ask the groups to take on the following roles:
- Customer;
- Customer's companion (wife, husband, friend, child);
- Shop assistant;
- Shop manager.

Tell the children that the customer is making a complaint in a shop. Discuss with the children what this complaint could be about – for example, poor service, poor display, over-heated shop, lack of customer facilities (toilets, cafeteria etc), non-availability of goods, returning unwanted or faulty goods. Let the customers and companions decide what they would like to complain about, and let each group act out the events that follow.

Follow-up
Discuss the roles and responsibilities of service industries. Is the customer always right? What are the customer's rights? What are the shop's rights?

Visit a shop and talk with the workers and the manager. Invite your local Trading Standards Officer to visit the class and talk with the children about the scenarios used in their dramas.

Production line

Age range
Seven to eleven.

Group size
Whole class.

What you need
Tables arranged in a line, a variety of art and craft materials, copies of photocopiable pages 126 to 127.

What to do
Use the instructions on pages 126 to 127 to set up a production line of 15 children to make masks. Ask the rest of the class to make the same item, but on an individual basis, as craftspeople who have the power to make decisions about the design of their product.

Explain to children that some factories are organised on a production line basis, and that they are taking on the roles of factory workers.

Certain situations may arise: for example a pile up of work at one point on the line because someone is not working quickly enough, complaints about tools or the boring nature of the jobs. Let the children deal with these problems as they arise.

Add complexity by appointing one child as quality controller, or by having a production line supervisor to iron out problems.

Follow-up
Discuss afterwards how it felt to be working on a production line. Did the children feel a sense of pride in their product? Did they enjoy their jobs? How does this compare with the children working individually? Who produced more items? Did the children on the production line behave differently from the children working individually? Which group talked more? Compare the products. What are the main differences between working on a production line and working individually?

Job interview

Age range
Nine to eleven.

Group size
Whole class, working in groups of four or five.

What you need
Job advertisements, application forms.

What to do
This drama activity could form part of a wider investigation into the processes of getting a job. Let the children examine advertisements and application forms, and find out what qualifications are needed for different jobs.

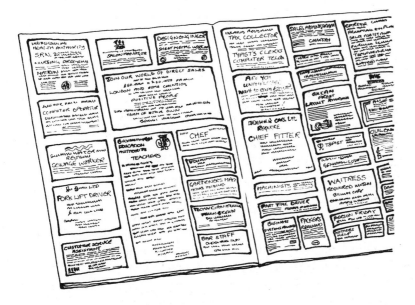

Ask each group to compile an advertisement for a job which other members of the class may apply for. Encourage them to consider what qualifications are needed, and whether to supply an application form or to require candidates to send a curriculum vitae.

When the advertisements are finished, display them and ask each child to write an application for one of them. Let them make up a character for themselves and decide their age, qualifications, interests and so on. Then let each group discuss the applications they have received, and draw up a short-list of suitable applicants.

Ask the groups to plan interview sessions. What questions will they need to ask? Discuss equal opportunities issues with the class. Point out that appointments cannot be made on grounds of sex, race or personal preference. The panel must refer to the job criteria which they listed earlier, and come to a fair decision which they can justify. Let the groups carry out interviews and decide which candidate to appoint.

Follow-up
Invite a manager from a local business to discuss the procedures the children designed, and compare these with the ones used in real companies.

Hard sell

Age range
Seven to eleven.

Group size
Whole class, working in pairs.

What you need
Props for a shop scene.

What to do
Ask one child in each pair to take on the role of salesperson in a shop. Explain that it is important to these shop assistants that they sell as much as possible because they get commission on each item sold, and as their income is low they need the money.

Ask the second child to be a customer. Let each child decide what sort of customer she wants to be: for example, dithery and unable to make decisions; very demanding; dissatisfied; a difficult size or shape which cannot easily be fitted.

Ask the pairs to develop their scenes, and at the end of the session perform them to the rest of the class.

Follow-up
Invite a shop assistant to visit the class and discuss positive and negative aspects of the job with the children.

Shipwrecks and disasters

This chapter is slightly different; the ideas here can be used together, in a sequence of your own choosing, to form a series of activities over several weeks. The first three ideas offer alternative scenarios for the action. Select one of these to begin with, and then choose as many of the rest as you need.

The activities are designed to allow children to develop ideas about how their own society might be organised. They are presented with incidents which require them to make joint decisions about how their group should operate. As in all role-play, children will bring to this their own observations and experiences of how their society works.

Scene-setters

Shipwrecked!

Age range
Seven to eleven.

Group size
Groups of about six, of mixed sex and ability.

What you need
A plank or bench, postcards, a nautical hat, a recording of storm music such as the storm from *The Flying Dutchman* by Wagner or sea-storm sound effects.

What to do
Tell the class that they are going on a school journey by sea. Ask them to line up to go on board (via the plank)

with their luggage, and meet the Captain (you). Let one child be the Purser and ask him to allocate a group to each cabin (a corner of the room).

Ask the children to unpack and prepare for the journey in their cabins. Announce daily routines, such as mealtimes and a life-boat drill. Let the children write postcards home.

After the routine has been established, use appropriate sound effects to introduce the build up of a storm. Finally announce that the ship is in danger of sinking. The passengers must abandon ship.

End the activity by telling the children that there's surf on the starboard side. Perhaps there's an island there!

Follow-up
Ask the children to make diaries of their voyage.

Follow this activity with 'What shall we rescue?' on page 100.

Aircrash

Age range
Seven to eleven.

Group size
Groups of about six, of mixed sex and ability.

What you need
A plank or bench, rows of chairs laid out as in an aircraft, a pilot's hat, a recording of storm sound effects.

What to do
Ask one group to assume the roles of aircraft cabin crew, and tell the rest of the class that they are going on a school journey by air, on a long distance flight. Let them line up to board the aircraft (via the plank) and meet the cabin crew. Ask the cabin crew to allocate seats.

Once in their seats, let the children prepare for the journey. Ask the cabin crew to announce routine arrangements for life-belts, oxygen masks etc. Introduce the following scenario.

The plane takes off, and the Captain gives details of the flight times, the altitude and, from time to time, where the plane is. It is night. Meals are served, and an in-flight movie begins.

After the routine has been established, the Captain's voice breaks in. The plane is over the Indian Ocean, and there's a major storm. The lights flicker. An announcement is made that the electrical circuits have failed, and the plane is losing height fast.

The Captain makes a final announcement: 'I intend to ditch the aircraft in the sea. I can see some surf down there – perhaps there's an island there . . .'

Follow-up
Ask the children to make diaries of their flight.

Follow this activity with 'What shall we rescue?' on page 100.

Lost in space

Age range
Seven to eleven.

Group size
Groups of about six, of mixed sex and ability.

What you need
Rows of seats, some space music such as *Also Sprach Zarathustra* by Richard Strauss.

What to do
Tell the class that they have been selected to journey to a distant planet to found a new settlement. Ask them to line up to go on board the spacecraft with their luggage, and meet the Captain (you). Let them form groups, each group sharing a cabin.

Act out the following scene.

In their cabins, the children unpack and prepare for the journey. The Captain announces daily routines, and the preparations for take-off. There's a countdown, and then sound effects for blast-off.

A routine for life on board the spacecraft is established. There are some emergency drills. The children make radio broadcasts back to Earth, describing their progress deep into space.

After the routine has been established, the Captain announces one day that the spacecraft engines have developed a fault; there's no need for concern, as repairs can be made. Later the Captain announces that the ship has been holed by a meteorite, and that each group must prepare to abandon ship in their landing module.

The final announcement is that there may be a small planet just within reach of the landing modules.

Follow-up
Ask the children to make diaries of their voyage.

Follow this activity with 'What shall we rescue?' on page 100.

Developing the action

What shall we rescue?

Age range
Seven to eleven.

Group size
Groups of about six, of mixed sex and ability.

What you need
No special equipment.

What to do
After using one of the activities on pages 97 to 99, give the groups the following brief.

Each group has just two minutes to select one item from the ship/aircraft/spacecraft that they can take with them. They must all agree on which item to take.

The vessel breaks up. Each group makes its way to their lifeboat/landing module with their object. As they leave, the ship sinks/aircraft sinks/spacecraft explodes. The groups make their way through the dark to the island/planet, and the children land in a state of exhaustion. No adults survive.

Follow-up
Continue the diaries, writing about the escape from the wrecked vessel.

Continue the drama with 'The first day' on page 101.

The first day

Age range
Seven to eleven.

Group size
Groups of about six, of mixed sex and ability.

What you need
No special equipment.

What to do
Tell the children that it is now day-break on the island or planet. They can now explore their surroundings. There are no other people on the island or planet. Are there any dangerous animals? Are there cliffs and marshes? What foods are available? What materials are available?

Ask each group to decide on what their priorities are. What two or three things do they think they must do in the first day?

When the groups have reached their decisions, take them out of role and discuss *how* each group came to a decision. Did they have a vote? Did they choose a leader to decide for them? How did they settle their differences?

In any group, there are likely to be different ideas and opinions. What is important is that people are able to put forward different ideas and to come to acceptable decisons. This does not necessarily mean having a leader.

Follow-up
Ask the children to write diaries for the day. Ask them to make models of the locality, showing the resources.

Continue the drama with other activities in this section.

101

Sharing out the jobs

Age range
Seven to eleven.

Group size
Groups of about six, of mixed sex and ability.

What you need
Large sheets of paper, coloured pens.

What to do
Tell the groups that they must think about all the different tasks that they will have to tackle over the next few weeks. What jobs have to be done? What are the priorities?

Encourage discussion to ensure that all the groups think of food-gathering, shelter, protection, cleaning, cooking, building, keeping warm etc.

How will the groups decide which jobs have to be done first? How will they share out the jobs?

Ask each group to agree on and list all the jobs that there are, and then to sort them into order of importance. How often will each job need to be done? Who will do which job?

Let the groups make charts of daily and weekly tasks. Encourage them to act out some of the tasks.

Follow-up
Discuss how the groups shared the work out. Did they look at particular individuals' skills, or simply share things out? Did girls get stereotyped jobs? Do they accept this?

Who needs rules?

Age range
Seven to eleven.

Group size
Groups of about six, of mixed sex and ability.

What you need
Paper, pens.

What to do
Withdraw one member from each group, and tell them that they are going to refuse to do the job or jobs they have been given. They are to argue that they don't see why they should do what anyone else asks them to do.

Ask each group to decide what it is going to do about this. Help them to tackle the issues in some sort of order. For example:

- Should the group make up rules?
- How would they make rules?
- What will they do if the rules are not followed?

If the children decide to make rules, encourage them to write them down and display them.

Follow-up
Develop this activity by arranging a trial to decide whether someone has broken the rules or not.

Organise an activity which tests the justice of the rules a group has made, so that they see the need for drafting rules very carefully.

Time out

Age range
Seven to eleven.

Group size
Groups of about six, of mixed sex and ability.

What you need
No special equipment.

What to do
Tell the children that it's leisure time on the island/
planet. What do the members of each group want to
do? Let each group have a meeting to decide.

What if one group member wants to do something
potentially dangerous, perhaps exploring a hazardous
area? If they are injured, or even killed, who will have to
do their work?

Ask the groups to decide whether they need rules to
prevent their members doing things that might affect the
work and safety of the rest of the group.

Follow-up
Discuss laws discouraging people from undertaking
dangerous activities.

Lean times

Age range
Seven to eleven.

Group size
Groups of about six, of mixed sex and ability.

What you need
No special equipment.

What to do
Tell the groups that food supplies are short, but those children in the group whose job it is to collect food demand more than an equal share of what's left. Brief them to say that this is because they need the energy to gather the food. They might also argue that it's only fair that they get most, because they do the work in getting it.

Is this fair? Let each group argue how the food will be divided.

Follow-up
Discuss what is meant by 'fair'. Arguments about the fairness of sharing out the rewards of work have been recorded from earliest history: the topic will keep your class in discussion as long as you let it.

Swap shop

Age range
Seven to eleven.

Group size
Groups of about six, of mixed sex and ability.

What you need
Craft materials such as clay, balsa wood and card.

What to do
Encourage the groups to make items which they can use. Ask one to make clay pots for cooking and water carrying; another to make wooden sledges for dragging firewood and a third to make (miniature) garments, etc.

Explain that the groups can make these items because they each have particular skills, and because they have particular access to the raw materials. For example, perhaps the pot-making group has set up base on clay soil.

If all the groups need all the items, how can they arrange to exchange things? Can they arrange a bartering system?

This may work initially as a straight swapping session. But what happens subsequently when some items wear out or break faster than others? How might the groups then manage to trade?

Who's in charge?

Age range
Seven to eleven.

Group size
Groups of about six, of mixed sex and ability.

What you need
No special equipment.

What to do
Brief one child in each group to say that he wishes to leave and start his own group, with himself as leader. These children must try to persuade others to join them and accept their leadership.

This activity should produce a series of tensions that will need to be discussed. Different groups may be organised in different ways, and both those with established leaders and those which share leadership will find this a challenge.

It is often worth encouraging the groups to discuss whether leaders are necessary; and if so, how they should be chosen.

Many groups will actively base their discussions on what they know about parliamentary procedures.

Treasure trove

Age range
Seven to eleven.

Group size
Groups of about six, of mixed sex and ability.

What you need
A bag of toy coins for each group.

What to do
Take aside a couple of children in each group and tell them that they have discovered a sack of gold coins.

They must consider what they will do with their find. If they try to conceal it, let the others in the group know that the pair have found something.

The discussions will probably initially centre on the notion of sharing and fairness. When this seems to have been sorted out, ask the group what is the value of the coins? The coins can only be of value if everyone agrees on a rate of exchange. Will they do this? How will they determine the value?

Follow-up
If they do use the money for exchanging for goods, let another child discover another hoard of coins, even larger than the first. The effect of flooding the market with more currency should produce an interesting and sudden devaluation!

The great escape

Age range
Seven to eleven.

Group size
Groups of about six, of mixed sex and ability.

What you need
No special equipment.

What to do
Tell the groups that they have found a possible means of escaping from the island/planet. This might be a raft, or a supply of fuel for the landing module.

What should they do? Should they try to escape, or wait for a rescue party? If they go, what preparations will be needed?

In some groups, this might precipitate a division of opinion. Let the children campaign for their views in various ways, and even have elections based on the issue.

Follow-up
End the sequence of activities with the group's successful escape or rescue. Encourage them to write the full story of their adventures.

Performance

Many adults have memories of having to perform in front of others when they were children. These memories are often strong because the experience was either particularly successful or particularly traumatic. It is important to ensure that performances are a positive experience for the children taking part and not just for the audience.

Performances can grow out of classroom drama sessions; they should not be seen as something separate. Improvisations can be scripted and developed for assemblies or for performance to parents. It is also valuable for children to use material written by other people, which can act as a model for their own writing.

In putting on a performance children encounter many aspects of drama which are not involved in workshop drama: costumes, more props and, above all, acting to an audience.

I liked that play

Age range
Seven to eleven.

Group size
Whole class.

What you need
Flip chart, large pieces of sugar paper, felt-tipped pens.

What to do
This activity is particularly effective if the children have just been to see a play at a theatre or have had a visit from a theatre company in school.

Talk to the children about any plays and performances they have seen. Were the occasions enjoyable? Get them to identify what it was that made it a good or bad performance. Encourage the children to think critically and to avoid comments like 'It was just good', or 'I just liked it'. Help them to identify what it was that made the play good. Was it because they like comedy or adventure, was it the acting, the story-line, the costumes or the music?

When the children have decided what they particularly liked about the play, look at this aspect in greater detail. For example, if a particular character is mentioned, look at the attributes of that character. Was she like someone they know, or a comic character, or larger than life? Look at the different scenes that together make the story. Can the children pick out the main action of each scene? Compare and contrast scenes with a large amount of activity with those that are quieter. See how the story-line moves along through these different scenes. Where is the climax of the play? How did the play start or finish? Were the endings or beginnings successful? Would the children have liked a different ending? Children might like to suggest alternative endings.

Treading the boards

Age range
Seven to eleven.

Group size
Whole class.

What you need
A local theatre, books about the theatre, pens, paper.

What to do
Arrange a visit to a local theatre and look at the different jobs involved, such as box office, promotions, catering, stage managing, lighting, costumes, scriptwriting. The theatre might have an education officer who can organise a tour of the theatre and arrange meetings with some of the people who work there. Arrange for the children to interview people with a range of different jobs and roles.

If a visit is not possible, get the children to talk about any previous theatre visits they have made. Encourage them to read about the theatre using reference books from the library. Ask them to draw up a list of jobs in the theatre.

Get the children to work out the sequence of roles that is needed before a performance can take place. Does the box office sell tickets before or after the catering manager orders the food? Do the posters go up before the play starts rehearsals? Who pays the expenses before the money is collected from the sale of tickets?

Follow-up
Introduce the idea of a classroom theatre company and discuss roles. Is it possible to replicate in the classroom every job that is essential to a theatre? Which ones will have to be omitted? Most schools, for example, would not have stage lighting. What sort of refreshments are feasible in a school? Help the children to decide which role to take.

While this is being planned and implemented, organise a performance of some kind. You could either have two groups, one performing and the other doing the behind-the-scenes jobs, or double up and let each child be involved in both areas. The performance could be with puppets, or it might be a talent show or a play.

It's a myth

Age range
Seven to eleven.

Group size
Whole class.

What you need
Books of Greek myths and legends, lengths of fabric, card, scissors, paints.

What to do
Tell the children a Greek legend, such as the story of King Midas or the Minotaur. Get the children to discuss how this could be presented to another class or as an assembly.

Help the children to decide on parts, props and simple costumes. Lengths of material are easily made into tunics, and card masks for the upper part of the face are effective and easy to make. Complement the drama with paintings and models.

The following Greek myths and legends could be used:
- King Midas and the golden touch;
- Daedalus and Icarus;
- Pandora's box;
- The adventures of Perseus;
- Theseus and the Minotaur;
- Jason and the Argonauts.

Follow-up
There are many excellent stories from other cultures which make ideal subjects for similar activities. Look out for stories of Rama and Sita or Hanuman the monkey

god, from India, Anansi from the Caribbean, and a variety of creation stories from different cultures. The *New Larousse Encyclopedia of Mythology* (Hamlyn) is a good source of legends.

Puppet show

Age range
Five to eleven.

Group size
Groups of about six.

What you need
Materials for puppet-making.

What to do
Select a number of children's own stories. Divide the children into groups and get them to make puppets representing the characters in one of the stories. The kinds of puppet they make will depend upon the age of the children.

Finger puppets
Help the children cut out small pieces of felt or thick paper, and sew or stick them together. Draw on some faces and costumes with felt-tipped pens, or cut out features from felt or paper and stick these on to the finger puppets.

Sock puppets
Help the children to embroider facial features on to clean unwanted socks, or sew on buttons for eyes and wool for hair. Let the children add clothes and other features made from scraps of fabric.

Glove puppets
Help the children to cut out a glove puppet shape from fabric, and then stick or sew the two parts together. They can add features and decorations as with the sock puppets.

Paper bag puppets
These are ideal if you want puppets for immediate use which do not need to last very long. Ask the children to draw faces on plain paper bags, and stick on hair, ears and other features. Fit the bags over the children's wrists and secure them in place with string or elastic bands.

Rod puppets

Let the children make puppet heads by inflating balloons and covering them with papier mâché. Make sure that the balloons have several layers all over. Children will find it easier to cover the balloons evenly if they use alternate layers of newspaper and white paper. They can then see which areas have not been covered.

Allow the papier mâché to dry between sessions, and do not let the children try to build up too many layers at once. Encourage them to use the paper to build up facial features, horns, tusks, beaks and snouts, rather than painting them on afterwards.

When the first layers are dry, attach a narrow cardboard tube to the tied end of the balloon, and secure it with adhesive tape. Continue building up the layers of papier mâché, making sure that they cover the tube and hold it in place.

When the papier mâché layers are finished and have dried completely, burst the balloon and push a stick into the head through the tube, attaching it to the tube with adhesive tape.

Paint the heads, and finish them with a coat of wood varnish. When this is dry the children can add hair, hats and jewellery.

Make costumes for the puppets from a doubled piece of fabric. Make sure that a child's hand will be able to fit into the fabric and move freely when it is sewn up. Cut out hands or paws as appropriate and attach them to the arms of the garments. Then sew the garments up and stick the costumes to the heads.

When the puppets are complete, help the children to dramatise their stories.

A simple puppet theatre can be built from large cardboard boxes, stuck together and covered with paper. Stage blocks can be used in the same way.

The moral is . . .

Age range
Five to eleven.

Group size
Groups of about four.

What you need
A book of Aesop's fables, puppets.

What to do
Read some of Aesop's fables to the children, such as 'The Lion and the Mouse', 'The Fox and the Crow', 'The Town Mouse and the Country Mouse' and 'The Boy Who Cried Wolf'. Ask the children to use puppets to act out one of the fables. Let older children try to think of a modern human equivalent of one of the stories.

The fables can be woven together into a single performance. Help the children to think of an effective way of doing this. Should one of the animals act as compère? Could a story be used to link the different plays together? Perhaps Aesop could be the story-teller and introduce his plays to the children. Choose some suitable music to link the plays together.

Assembly

Age range
Five to eleven.

Group size
Whole class or groups.

What you need
A large space.

What to do
Drama can be an interesting and lively way of conveying information, whether in class or to a larger audience, as in a school assembly.

Most projects can incorporate some drama. Think of lively ways of presenting a scientific principle, such as gravity, or a piece of history like the Gunpowder Plot, or a question of health, such as the need for exercise. Younger children could try to illustrate a simple mathematical concept, like odds and evens or shape. Older ones could present more sophisticated concepts such as facts about electricity, force or place value. The children can put together short scenes which illustrate what they have learnt. These do not need to be complicated or lengthy.

Encourage the children to think up ideas for themselves. How could they make this subject more meaningful to children who have not done the classwork? What would have helped them to understand a particular concept better?

Rehearse the performance and present it as part of the class assembly.

Musical thoughts

Age range
Seven to eleven.

Group size
Groups of four children.

What you need
A selection of tapes and a cassette player with earphones.

What to do
Play a variety of pieces of music to the class. Discuss with them how the different pieces convey contrasting atmospheres and effects. Does the music make them feel sad, excited, calm? What does it make them think of – flight, danger, loss?

Explain that you want to build up a collection of music to enhance their performances and assemblies. With a cassette player and earphones ask a group of up to four children to listen to tapes and select pieces of music which give particular effects; frightening music, sad music, peaceful music etc. When they have found a piece, play it to the rest of the class to see if they agree. Add these pieces to your collection. This can be a continuing activity.

Some useful music might be:
- Carnival of the Animals – Saint Saëns
- Bolero – Ravel
- The Seasons – Vivaldi
- The Planet Suite – Holst
- Canon in D Major – Pachelbel
- Carmina Burana – Orff
- Tubular Bells – Mike Oldfield
- Cacharpaya – Incantation

A wider audience

Age range
Seven to eleven.

Group size
Whole class or large group.

What you need
The support of a local old peoples' home or hospital.

What to do
If you have material from a successful assembly, a short play, or scenes from the celebration of a festival, why not consider sharing these with people outside school who may not be able to get out of their own environment because of illness or disability?

Short plays, musical items and festival celebrations are particularly welcomed by institutions. A preliminary visit, during which you outline your plans and what you have to offer, is essential. Make sure you know what they expect in terms of such things as times, numbers

expected, the room to be used etc. Check that you know where to meet, where toilets are situated and where the children can change. Decide on the length and programme for your performance. Remember that old or sick people tire easily.

Brief the children thoroughly. They will be performing in a different place and under very different circumstances. They may find the environment of a hospital or home uncomfortable. Draw up a check-list and ensure that you take all the equipment and materials you need.

Follow-up
Was the visit a success? What did the audience seem to like best? Is it possible to carry out some market research and find out what sort of performance appeals most to this audience? If the response is favourable, develop these links and return to talk to the people in the institution and put up posters advertising your next visit.

Opportunity knocks

Age range
Nine to eleven.

Group size
Groups of about six.

What you need
Simple props.

What to do
Talk to the children about a compilation show. This might be a talent show with a child acting as compère introducing the different acts, or a series of short acts linked together round a theme. The theme might be a journey where different incidents or adventures occur, a visit to another world where they meet a variety of different (friendly!) creatures, or a disastrous series of family visits to various relatives.

Give the children time to practise in their groups what they want to do. They will need several practice sessions, and help and advice from you. Remind them of the elements of a successful performance. It is best to keep the acts short and to stop children from getting too carried away with the limelight!

Drama festival

Age range
Seven to eleven.

Group size
Whole school, working in classes.

What you need
A large space.

What to do
An exciting focus for children's acting is a drama festival. This might take place during a Book Week or as part of a school celebration such as a centenary.

Let each class devise and perform a small play for the rest of the school. If part of Book Week, it might be based on a book, or it could be a different version of a well-known story, such as a traditional fairy story with a surprise ending. If the performance is for a special school event, the plays could be connected to this event, such as a dramatisation of events in the school's past. Alternatively the plays could be built around a theme, or the choice could be left entirely free.

Keep the entries simple, with minimum props and a time limit. Make sure that all children are involved in some way. Make posters, and advertise the different plays around the school.

Fix a date for the children to perform their plays. It is usually best to allow the younger children to perform first. You might like to invite parents too. This could be used as a fund-raising event.

Freeze!

Age range
Seven to eleven.

Group size
Large group or whole class.

What you need
A large space.

What to do
With suitable music and good costumes and props, a tableau is a simple but effective way of portraying a scene such as the Nativity or a Rama and Sita story. Let some of the children narrate the story while others move into place until a complete picture is built up. If possible, create a stage out of blocks or low PE equipment, so that the tableau has shape. Position the children for maximum effect.

Another idea is to use music and poetry based on a theme. Help the children to choose poems or writings on a theme such as peace or friendship. Read the poems several times, and ask the children to suggest movements or mime that would illustrate the meaning of the words. Practise putting words and movements together.

Then think about suitable music to enhance the performance. If you have tried 'Musical thoughts' on page 118 you will already have a store of music to choose from.

Finally, put the words, music and movement together. Ask the children to move into position to the background of the readings and the music, miming to the words and then 'freezing' into the tableau. Keep the theme simple and the performance short. If you have stage lighting of any sort, this would add dramatically to the effect.

Reproducible material

Park workers

Your job includes weed control in the park. This is partly done by hand-weeding, but most of the weeding is done with chemical weed-killers, which have to be sprayed on paths and lawns.

One of you has recently attended a park workers' conference, and in conversation with park workers from another area, you discover that their local authority has banned the use of one particular weed-killing chemical on the grounds that it may be dangerous both for the workers who use it and for the general public.

Union health and safety representative

You are a park worker who has been elected to be the local health and safety representative of your union. Your role involves identifying dangers caused by tools, materials or unsafe working practices. You have to draw these to the attention of the management, and negotiate possible solutions.

Park manager

You are employed by the local council to be responsible for the park. You are responsible for managing the park budget, for employing and directing park workers, and for ordering materials and equipment.

Weed-killers are used in the park because they save money. Many more park workers would have to be employed to do all the weeding by hand, and you would not be able to afford their wages on your budget. You are aware that in general the workers prefer to use chemicals because this involves less heavy labour than weeding by hand.

Members of the public

You use the local park regularly, for different purposes: walking the dog, taking the children out to play, jogging, sunbathing. Decide exactly what role each of you will take.

Decide, too, how you get to hear about the weed-killer issue. For example, is it from a relative who is a park worker, from the local newspaper, or because you have noticed ill effects after sitting on the grass?

You decide to talk to the park manager about your concerns.

This page may be photocopied for use in the classroom and should not be declared in any return in respect of any photocopying licence.

Production line, see page 93

1. **Task**
   Draw the outline of the mask, adding round holes for eyes and mouth.

   Materials needed
   Template of mask, pencil, supply of card cut to size.

2. **Task**
   Cut out the main shape of the mask, following outline drawn.

   Materials needed
   Scissors.

3. **Task**
   Cut out the mouth.

   Materials needed
   Small scissors with sharp points.

4. **Task**
   Cut out the right eye.

   Materials needed
   Small scissors with sharp points.

5. **Task**
   Cut out the left eye.

   Materials needed
   Small scissors with sharp points.

6. **Task**
   Draw features in black as shown.

   Materials needed
   Black felt-tipped pen.

7. **Task**
   Colour in red lips.

   Materials needed
   Red felt-tipped pen.

8. **Task**
   Colour in eyelids green.

   Materials needed
   Green felt-tipped pen.

9. **Task**
   Colour in cheeks pink. Pass the mask on to number 11.

   Materials needed
   Pink felt-tipped pen.

10. **Task**
    Cut pieces of wool into short lengths for hair.

    Materials needed
    Balls of wool, scissors.

11. **Task**
    Stick wool on to the mask to form hair. Pass the mask on to number 14.

    Materials needed
    Adhesive.

12. **Task**
    Draw round template for nose shape. If you have time, help cut out noses and fold them to shape.

    Materials needed
    Template for nose, pencil, scissors.

13. **Task**
    Cut out card for the nose, and fold it into shape.

    Materials needed
    Scissors.

14. **Task**
    Stick nose on to face, by gluing the flaps.

    Materials needed
    Adhesive.

15. **Task**
    Use adhesive tape to attach string to either side of the mask to tie it around the head.

    Materials needed
    String, scissors, adhesive tape.

Notes
This production line is for fifteen children. You can easily lengthen it by designing more colouring to be done on the masks, or shorten it by combining or cutting out jobs.

This page may be photocopied for use in the classroom and should not be declared in any return in respect of any photocopying licence.

Production line, see page 93

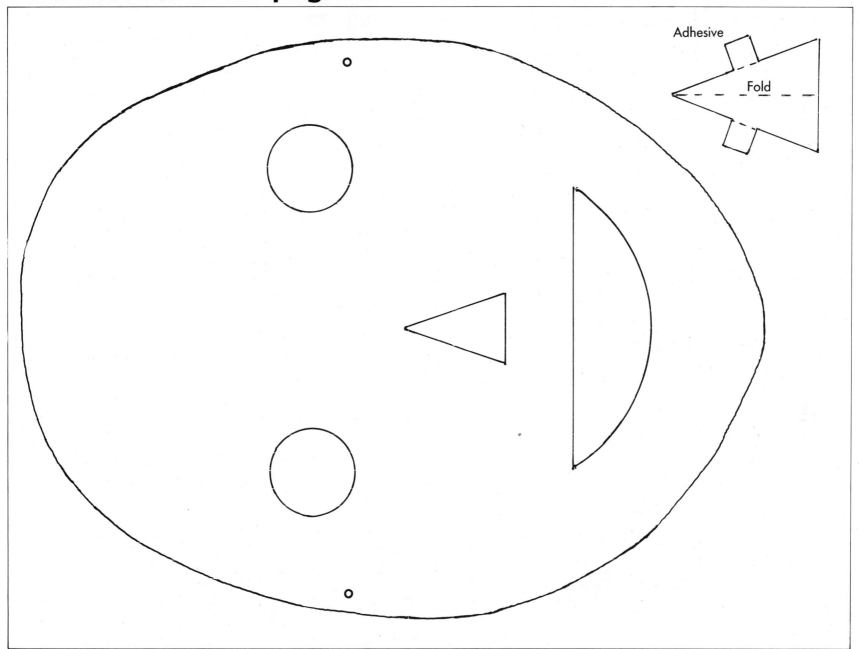

Adhesive

Fold

This page may be photocopied for use in the classroom and should not be declared in any return in respect of any photocopying licence.

Other Scholastic books

Bright Ideas
The *Bright Ideas* books provide a wealth of resources for busy primary school teachers. There are now more than 20 titles published, providing clearly explained and illustrated ideas on topics ranging from *Writing* and *Maths Activities* to *Assemblies* and *Christmas Art and Craft*. Each book contains material which can be photocopied for use in the classroom.

Management Books
The *Management Books* are designed to help teachers to organise their time, classroom and teaching more efficiently. The books deal with topical issues, such as *Parents and Schools* and organising and planning *Project Teaching*, and are written by authors with lots of practical advice and experiences to share.

Let's Investigate
Let's Investigate is an exciting range of photocopiable activity books giving open-ended investigative tasks.

Designed to cover the 6 to 12-year-old age range these books are ideal for small group or individual work. Each book presents progressively more difficult concepts and many of the activities can be adapted for use throughout the primary school. Detailed teacher's notes outlining the objectives of each photocopiable sheet and suggesting follow-up activities have been included.